IRAN:

Exposing the Latest Terrorist Game Plan of the IRGC-Quds Force

Formation of Proxy Naval Units

Published by

NATIONAL COUNCIL OF RESISTANCE OF IRAN

U.S. REPRESENTATIVE OFFICE (NCRI-US)

IRAN: Exposing the Latest Terrorist Game Plan of the IRGC-Quds Force
Formation of Proxy Naval Units

Copyright © National Council of Resistance of Iran – U.S. Representative Office, 2022.

First published in 2022
by National Council of Resistance of Iran — U.S. Representative Office (NCRI-US),
1747 Pennsylvania Ave., NW, Suite 1125, Washington, DC 20006

ISBN-10 (paperback): 1-944942-50-5
ISBN-13 (paperback): 978-1-944942-50-2

ISBN-10 (e-book): 1-944942-51-3
ISBN-13 (e-book): 978-1-944942-51-9

ISBN-10 (audiobook): 1-944942-52-1
ISBN-13 (audiobook): 978-1-944942-52-6

Library of Congress Control Number: 2022931928

Library of Congress Cataloging-in-Publication Data

National Council of Resistance of Iran — U.S. Representative Office.

IRAN: Exposing the Latest Terrorist Game Plan of the IRGC-Quds Force
Formation of Proxy Naval Units

1. Iran. 2.Yemen. 3.IRGC. 4.Terrorism. 5.Red Sea.

First Edition: February 2022
Printed in the United States of America

Table of Contents

Executive summary

According to information received from the network inside Iran of the main Iranian opposition, the People's Mojahedin Organization of Iran (PMOI), also referred to as the Mujahedin-e Khalq (MEK), the Islamic Revolutionary Guard Corps' Quds Force (IRGC-QF) has been recruiting mercenaries for newly created, armed and trained terrorist units to attack ships and maritime targets in the region. The IRGC-QF is the IRGC's extraterritorial arm.

After the elimination of Qassem Soleimani in January 2020, which weakened the Quds Force's ability to directly encroach in the countries of the region, the IRGC's capacity to intrude in Iraq, Lebanon and Syria has been on the decline. To compensate for this failure, the IRGC has turned to intervention in Yemen, especially escalating naval terrorist activities and threatening the international shipping on its shores.

The command headquarters of the Quds Force in Yemen recruits Houthi forces and sends them to Iran for training, where the IRGC-QF conducts training in specialized naval courses for its Yemeni, Iraqi, Syrian, Lebanese, and African mercenaries, who are then dispatched to their home countries to form proxy naval units.

The primary location for naval commando training for these proxy naval units is called the Khamenei Academy of Naval Sciences and Technology in Ziba Kenar on the Caspian coastline in Gilan Province. There is a section in the Khamenei Academy dedicated to the six-month training course of foreign mercenaries affiliated with the Quds Force. In January 2020, for example, one such course in naval science and technology was launched for about 200 Yemeni mercenaries.

Several Persian Gulf islands are being used for maritime training for IRGC-QF mercenaries, including Farur and Qeshm islands. The IRGC Navy has several centers in different parts of Qeshm

Island, considered one of the main training complexes of the Quds Force. In addition to training the IRGC Navy and foreign terrorist forces, the IRGC has stockpiled weapons and missiles at the island's underground facilities.

The Quds Force has set up a smuggling network to provide weapons and equipment to its proxies for naval attacks. One of the methods of transferring weapons to Yemen is to use third countries, such as Somalia. Another means is using small boats along the coasts of the Sea of Oman. One of the most important ports used for this purpose is Bandar-e-Jask.

The Quds Force has equipped the Houthis with speedboats, missiles, mines, and other weapons. It employs tactics that utilize speedboats and asymmetric warfare — similar to those used by the IRGC's Navy in the Persian Gulf — to expand conflicts into the Arabian Sea, Bab al-Mandab, and the Red Sea. Many terrorist operations in this region targeting foreign and Arab ships have been carried out by these proxy naval units. In this way, the Iranian regime covers its tracks, and pursues its agenda under the shadow of the Houthi war in the region.

Since early 2021, and more so since August 2021, when Ebrahim Raisi took office as the new president of the Iranian regime, Tehran has stepped up its maritime terrorist operations using its foreign mercenaries, especially the Houthis. This escalation is in line with its stepped-up drone attacks against the Persian Gulf countries, as well as its nuclear defiance.

The continued offers of concessions by Western countries and lack of accountability for the Iranian regime's terrorist operations as well as its killings at home, have emboldened Tehran to step up its rogue behavior creating mayhem in the region. Regardless of what the Iranian regime might do with its nuclear weapons program and its negotiations with the P5+1, Tehran must be held accountable for its proxy war in the region, its terrorism, its development of ballistic missiles, and its egregious violations of human rights and suppression of Iranian citizens engaged in ongoing protests.

Tehran's latest game plan to advance its terrorist agenda by prioritizing mercenaries and stepping up regional mayhem is intended to project power and cover its fundamental weakness inside Iran. Since December 2017, there have been eight major uprisings, as well as successive protests by various sectors of Iranian society urgently desiring fundamental change. The regime hopes that this image will provide additional leverage internationally and domestically, and explains why it is investing lavish amounts of money and resources for training, funding and arming its proxies, while a vast majority of the Iranian people live below the poverty line.

Any conciliatory approach, especially since Raisi has taken office, would lead to Tehran's increased defiance. Therefore, none of the sanctions against the regime should be lifted. To the contrary, additional sanctions are warranted as a result of the Iranian regime's escalation of violence in the region and stepped-up repression at home.

Introduction

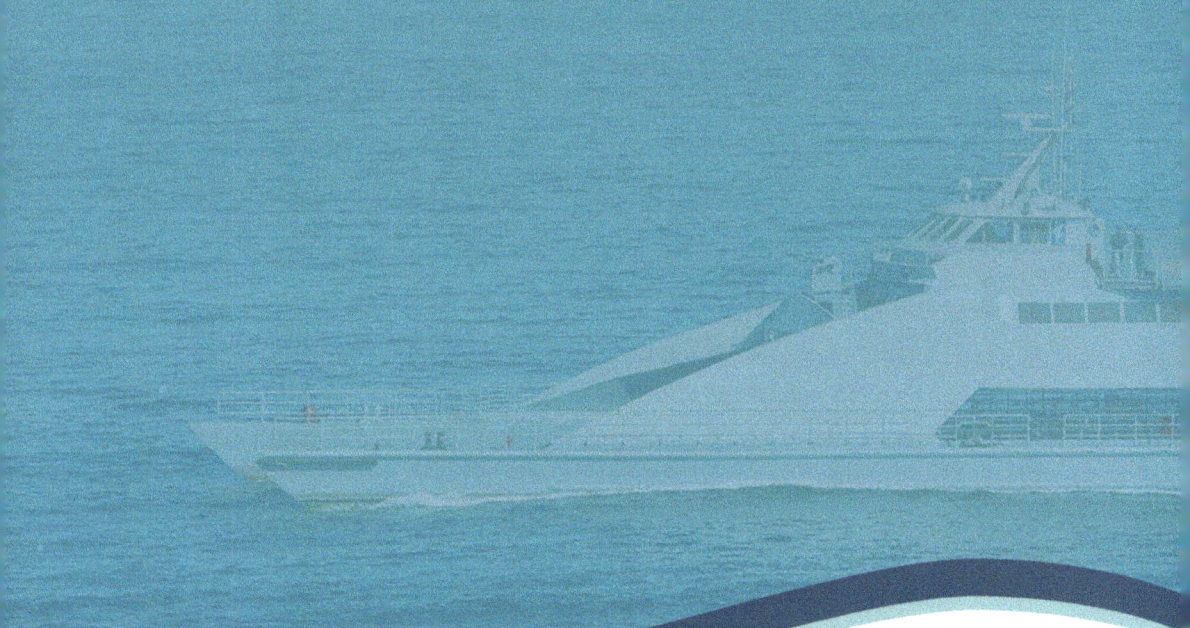

O ver the past year, 2021, the United States and European governments showed considerable flexibility to reach an agreement with the Iranian regime regarding the Iran Deal. The EU representative even oddly attended the inauguration of Ebrahim Raisi, the infamous henchman of the 1988 massacre of 30,000 political prisoners, who had been installed as president in a widely boycotted election.

Nevertheless, the regime has dashed to expand its program to obtain nuclear weapons, accelerated its warmongering in various countries, and equipped its mercenary militias with a variety of weapons, including unmanned aerial vehicles (UAVs). During the Vienna talks, the number of executions in Iran doubled compared to the same period last year.

Additionally, the regime is brazenly refusing to invest in improving the Iranian people's livelihood, welfare, health, education, employment or housing, further stoking public discontent. Khamenei, however, has more than doubled the budget of the IRGC to reinforce his police-military machine.

How to explain this behavior, ostensibly harmful to the regime itself? The explanation lies in the vulnerability of an unpopular ruling regime, attempting to ward off or at the very least delay its overthrow.

Since December 2017, there have been eight major uprisings, as well as successive protests by various sectors of Iranian society. The continuation of these uprisings is indicative of the discontent building from unresolved political, social, and economic problems. Iranian society urgently desires fundamental change.

The people are determined to overthrow the clerical regime, which lacks any semblance of legitimacy. Indeed, Supreme Leader Khamenei's first priority is to keep his regime in power. He has no solution to contain the uprisings, other than to enforce a vicious crackdown.

Through obtaining nuclear weapons, the regime seeks a way out of these crises. Advancing its terrorist agenda by prioritizing mercenaries and stepping up regional mayhem is intended to project power and cover its fundamental weakness inside Iran. Tehran hopes that this image will provide additional leverage internationally and domestically. This explains why the regime is investing lavish amounts of money and resources for training, funding and arming its proxies, while a vast majority of the Iranian people live below the poverty line.

This report focuses on one of the latest aspects of the regime's efforts to cover its fragile state as it fights for survival: the role of the IRGC's Quds Force in the formation of maritime terrorist units of foreign mercenaries.

Formation of proxy naval units by the IRGC-Quds Force

In the last few years, in conjunction with the expansion of the Islamic Revolutionary Guards Corps' (IRGC) terrorist activities in the Persian Gulf, the Sea of Oman and the Red Sea, the Quds Force of the IRGC (IRGC-QF) has increased its maritime activities.

According to information received from the network inside Iran of the main Iranian opposition, the People's Mojahedin Organization of Iran (PMOI/MEK), the Quds Force has been recruiting mercenaries for newly created, armed and trained terrorist units to attack ships and maritime targets in the region.

The IRGC-QF conducts training in specialized naval courses in Iran for its Yemeni, Iraqi, Syrian, Lebanese, and African mercenaries and dispatches them to their home countries to form naval units. Those established by the Quds Force in Yemen in particular carry out terrorist naval operations.

Details of the IRGC-QF's formation of terrorist naval units, including the cycle of recruitment and training for terrorist operations by proxy forces, as well as the cycle of sending weapons and other logistical support to them, are being revealed for the first time.

The strategy affords the politically weakened and vulnerable Iranian regime a veneer of plausible deniability for its proxy war in the region, as it seeks to augment the export of terrorism on which it depends.

After the elimination of Qassem Soleimani in January 2020, which weakened the Quds Force's ability to directly encroach in the countries of the region, the IRGC's capacity to intrude in Iraq, Lebanon and Syria has been on the decline. To compensate for this failure, the IRGC has turned to intervention in Yemen, especially escalating naval terrorist activities and threatening the international shipping on its shores.

The regime's adventurism in the Persian Gulf and the Sea of Oman regions has come with its benefits along with its political liability. The IRGC, therefore, has boosted its maritime threats in the Red Sea and the Bab al-Mandab Strait area using the Houthis, to enable it to marginalize its direct role in these actions. The naval terrorist operations in the Red Sea and the Bab al-Mandab Strait are supervised by the command headquarters of the Quds Force, but carried out by naval units established with Houthi forces.

The Bab al-Mandab Strait and Red Sea, where Quds Force naval units are focusing their terrorist operations

Stepping up naval terrorist operations during Raisi's tenure

Following Raisi's rise to power as president, the Iranian regime has stepped up its policy of export of terrorism, involving escalating operations by the IRGC's proxy forces, especially in Yemen. The leaders of the Houthis were among the first to congratulate the mullahs' president on his election. On August 4, 2021, Raisi hosted Houthi spokesman and chief negotiator, Mohammed Abdulsalam, in Tehran to personally express his regime's support for the Houthis.

On August 4, 2021, Raisi met in Tehran with a representative of the Yemeni Houthis, Mohammed Abdulsalam, to reiterate his support.

Some of the naval terrorist operations carried out by the Quds Force's affiliated militias in the Red Sea and on the coast of Yemen since Raisi took office as president in August 2021 are as follows:

- Attack by two boats carrying bombs on September 20, 2021 in the port of al-Saleef in the coastal province of Al-Hudaydah.

- Four suicide boat attacks on October 23, 2021 targeting the al-Jabanah beach camp in Al-Hudaydah.

- Attack by a suicide boat on November 8, 2021 on Al-Hudaydah beach.

- The detonation of 14 rounds of mines in the south of the Red Sea, considered a threat to international shipping, in the second week of November 2021.

- On December 7, 2021, the Justice Department announced the successful forfeiture of two large caches of the Iranian regime's arms, including 171 surface-to-air missiles and eight anti-tank missiles, destined for Houthi militants in Yemen. The U.S. Navy seized the weapons from two vessels in the Arabian Sea.[1]

- On December 20, the United States Navy's 5th Fleet seized upwards of 1,400 AK-47 assault rifles and 226,600 rounds of ammunition from a vessel originating from Iran. This ship was on a route historically used to illegally smuggle weapons to the Houthis in Yemen.[2]

- On January 3, 2022, the Houthis hijacked the Rawabi, a United Arab Emirates-flagged cargo vessel. The United Nations Security Council condemned the detention by the Houthis of the Emirati ship and asked the Houthis to release the ship and its crew.[3]

---

1   U.S. Department of Justice, "United States Prevails in Actions to Seize and Forfeit Iranian Terror Group's Missiles and Petroleum," December 7, 2021; https://www.justice.gov/opa/pr/united-states-prevails-actions-seize-and-forfeit-iranian-terror-group-s-missiles-and

2   U.S. Department of State, "Illegal Iranian Flow of Weapons to Yemen," Press Statement by Ned Price, Department Spokesperson, December 23, 2021; https://www.state.gov/illegal-iranian-flow-of-weapons-to-yemen/

3   "Security Council condemns Houthis' holding of UAE flagged ship," Saudi Gazette, January 15, 2022; https://saudigazette.com.sa/article/615889/World/America/Security-Council-condemns-Houthis-holding-of-UAE-flagged-ship

▶ Thousands of rocket launchers, machine guns, sniper rifles and other weapons seized in the Arabian Sea by the U.S. Navy likely originated from a single port in Iran (Jask), according to a confidential United Nations report that provides some of the most detailed evidence that Tehran is exporting arms to Yemen and elsewhere.[4]

▶ Arab Coalition spokesman Turki al-Maliki accused the Houthis of using Al-Hudaydah, Saleef and Ras Issa ports for military purposes — as workshops for assembling ballistic missiles and explosives-laden drone boats.[5]

Chart of Quds Force Recruitment, Dispatch and Training of Naval Terrorists

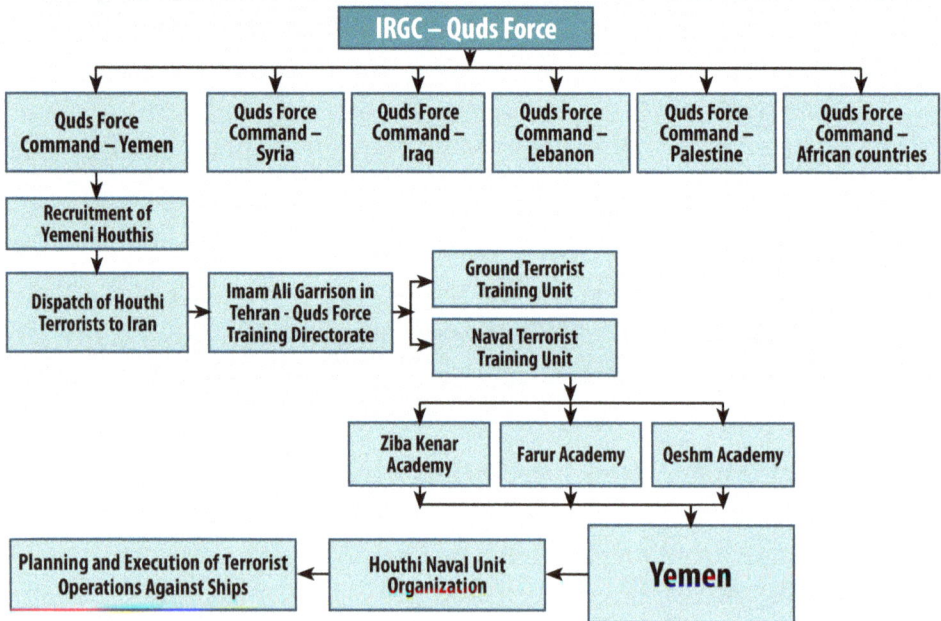

IRGC – Quds Force

| Quds Force Command – Yemen | Quds Force Command – Syria | Quds Force Command – Iraq | Quds Force Command – Lebanon | Quds Force Command – Palestine | Quds Force Command – African countries |

Recruitment of Yemeni Houthis

Dispatch of Houthi Terrorists to Iran → Imam Ali Garrison in Tehran - Quds Force Training Directorate → Ground Terrorist Training Unit / Naval Terrorist Training Unit

Ziba Kenar Academy | Farur Academy | Qeshm Academy

Planning and Execution of Terrorist Operations Against Ships ← Houthi Naval Unit Organization ← Yemen

4   Faucon, Benoit and Nissenbaum, Dion, Iran Navy Port Emerges as Key to Alleged Weapons Smuggling to Yemen, U.N. Report Says, The Wall Street Journal, January 9, 2022; https://www.wsj.com/articles/iran-navy-port-emerges-as-key-to-alleged-weapons-smuggling-to-yemen-u-n-report-says-11641651941

5   "UN demands access to Houthi-controlled port over 'military use' claim," Al-Mashareq and AFP, January 12, 2022; https://almashareq.com/en_GB/articles/cnmi_am/features/2022/01/12/feature-01

Recruiting terrorist candidates and dispatching them to Iran

The Quds Force Command operates bases in different countries of the region. With money and fundamentalist propaganda, the Quds Force recruits potential terrorists and dispatches them to Quds Force centers in Iran for terrorist training courses. The same method is used for proxy naval units.

In the past, the Quds Force Training Directorate had a naval training group which provided basic training, such as diving and sailing, to mercenaries. However, the IRGC has more recently formed the Quds Force Naval Unit in the context of the expansion of its terrorist activities by proxy forces in Iraq, Yemen, Syria, Palestine, Lebanon and several African countries. This Unit provides specialized (commando) training, and forms operational units to conduct naval warfare.

The Khamenei Academy of Naval Sciences and Technology

The primary location for naval commando training is at a naval academy called the Khamenei Academy of Naval Sciences and Technology in Ziba Kenar on the Caspian coastline in Gilan Province. This university was established in August 2013. Within four years, the university was expanded and all IRGC naval training, including that of IRGC-QF proxies, was transferred to this center. Mercenaries brought to Iran for naval training are sent back to their countries after receiving a six-month course.

Brig. Gen. Hassan Ali Zamani Pajooh

The first commander of the Quds Force Naval Unit in Ziba Kenar was Brig. Gen. Hassan Ali Zamani Pajooh, who was also the head of the Khamenei Academy until August 2019, when Second Admiral (Brigadier General) Abdolreza Dabestani was appointed as the president of the academy.

Zamani Pajooh is in charge of the naval training of foreign mercenaries of the Quds Force. He is currently the commander of a Quds Force barracks called Pazouki Garrison, which is the training ground for regional mercenaries.

Brig. Gen. Abdolreza Dabestani

Pazouki Garrison is located in Jalilabad, south of Tehran and east of Pishva city. He uses his office in the garrison to coordinate and resolve the issues and challenges of foreign mercenaries recruited for the Khamenei Academy.

The general location of the Pazouki Garrison south of Tehran

The Pazouki Garrison at Jalil Abad south of Tehran

Secret section at Khamenei Academy for foreign mercenary training

There is a section in the Khamenei Academy dedicated to the six-month training course of foreign mercenaries affiliated with the Quds Force. The dormitory of these terrorist recruits is separated from those of other students and no one is allowed contact with them in order to prevent leaks.

In January 2020, for example, a six-month training course was launched for about 200 Yemeni mercenaries who were trained in the academy. The next group was comprised of Iraqi mercenaries, whose training began in July 2020. After the completion of their terrorist training, the Iraqis were sent to al-Faw peninsula and Basrah to form a "naval unit" under the command of the Quds Force.

The Khamenei Academy's training section is headed by an IRGC functionary named Khademzadeh. The instructor for foreign mercenaries is IRGC Captain Seyyed Mehdi Hosseini, who is from Mazandaran Province.

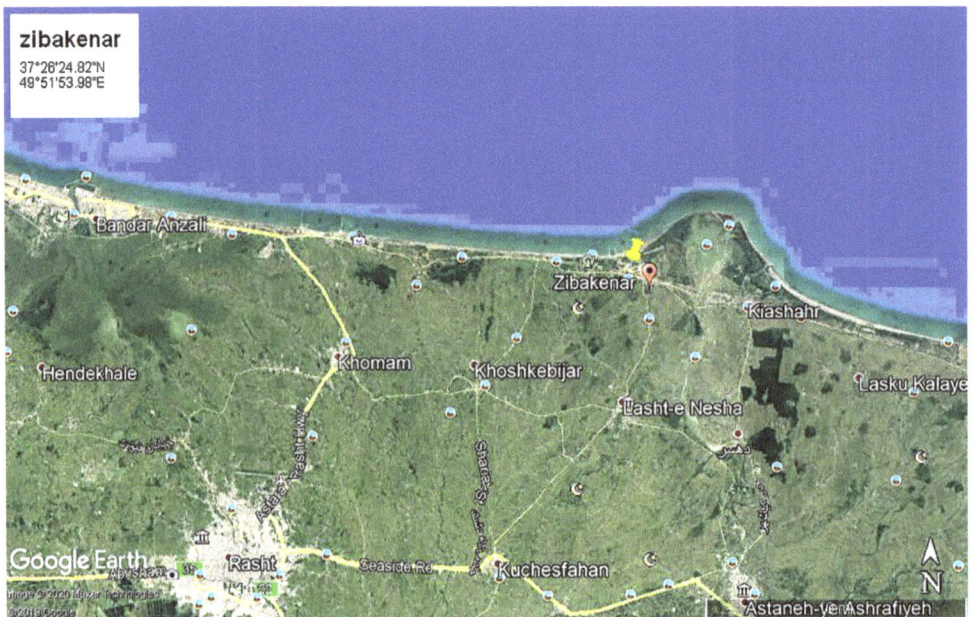

General area of the Khamenei Academy commando school

Perimeter of the IRGC commando university

Khamenei Academy in Ziba Kenar

Sections of the Khamenei Academy include:

1. The office of the sailing and navigation faculty

2. Warehouse for speedboats

3. Speedboat depot

4. Pier guard post

There are also two French yachts at the pier for naval reconnaissance.

Number 1 is Khamenei Academy commando school; 2, 3 and 4 are dormitories. The headquarters of the foreign mercenaries is located behind the commando school.

General naval training by the Quds Force Training Directorate

The Quds Force Training Directorate is one of the most important sections of the Quds Force. Its headquarters is located at Imam Ali Garrison, situated at the 20th kilometer of the Tehran-Karaj highway, Ardestani Boulevard, toward the end of Sarvan Street.

This directorate provides various military-terrorist training to mercenaries. A separate group from the IRGC provides general naval courses, such as diving and maritime training, in the cities of Ahvaz, Abadan and Qeshm.

Quds Force Training Directorate HQ at Imam Ali Garrison
at Tehran-Karaj Highway

Naval commando terrorist training base on Farur Island

Farur Island, which is a small, uninhabited island in the middle of the Persian Gulf, is under the control of the IRGC Navy and is one of its main channels for arms smuggling to Arab countries.

Farur Island is located to the north of Siri Island and southwest of Bandar Lengeh harbor, near Abu Musa Island. The distance from this island to the nearest coastal point of Hormozgan Province is about 20 km; it is 55 km from Kish Island.

The IRGC Navy commando brigade, called the Aba Abdullah Commandos Special Forces, is stationed on Farur Island. The March 23, 2017 operation against a British oil tanker was conducted by this brigade, which provides naval commando training to IRGC-affiliated terrorist mercenaries from Yemen and Bahrain.

The first commander of this brigade was an IRGC terrorist named Brigadier General Mohammad Nazeri, who was killed in the Persian Gulf in 2017. The current commander is Brigadier General Sadegh Amoui.

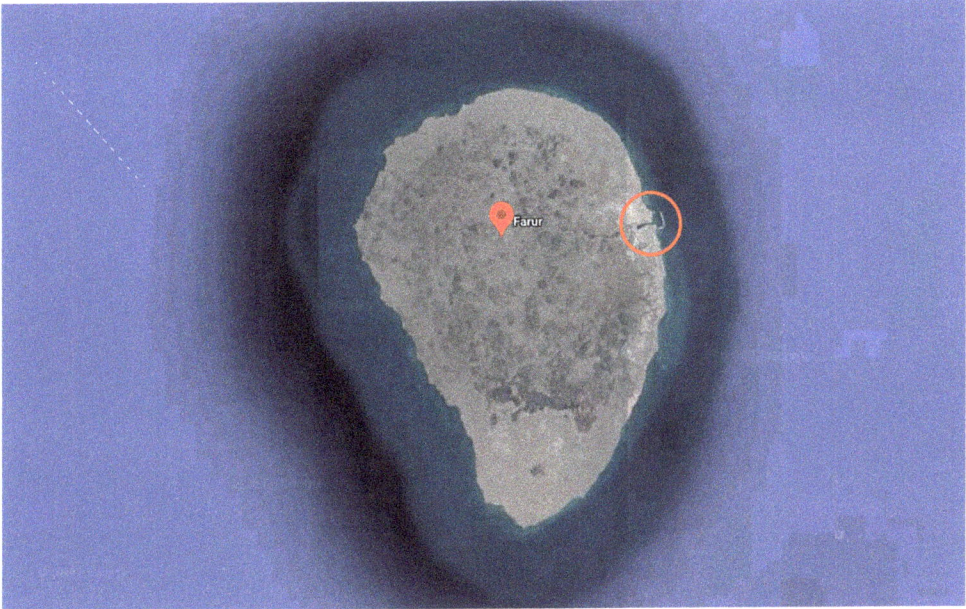

IRGC Navy commando brigade terrorist training base on Farur Island in the Persian Gulf

Marine training centers on Qeshm Island

The IRGC Navy has several centers in different parts of Qeshm Island, considered one of the training complexes of the Quds Force. In addition to training the IRGC Navy, these centers are also used to train foreign terrorist forces, to smuggle weapons into Gulf countries, and to illicitly smuggle goods and products.

According to information obtained, the IRGC has stockpiled weapons and missiles at the island's underground facilities. The command headquarters of the IRGC's 112th Zolfaqar naval brigade is located near Messen village on Qeshm Island.

IRGC marine training centers on Qeshm Island

The cycle of recruiting and training of proxy forces in Yemen

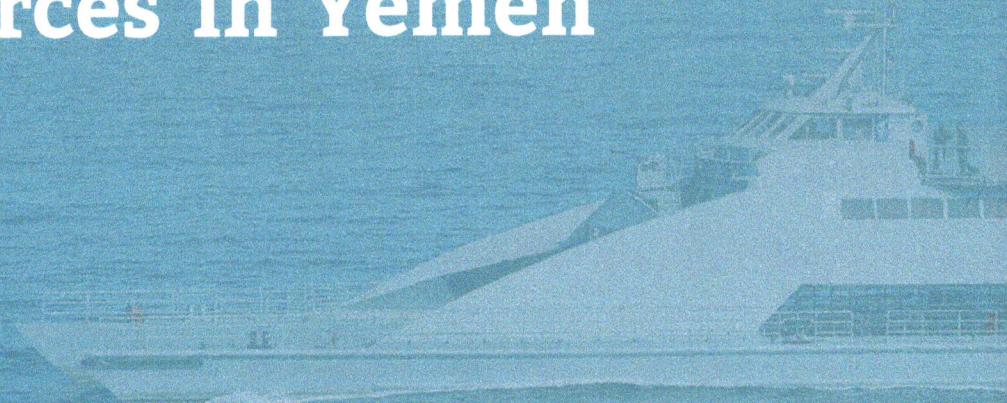

The Yemeni Houthis (Ansarullah) under the supervision of the Quds Force have waged a full-fledged proxy war with logistical, training, and weapons support provided by the Quds Force.

The Quds Force Command in Yemen dispatches its Houthi mercenaries to Iran for naval terrorist operations and commando training, and to organize them for operational purposes to fulfill the terrorist objectives of the Quds Force.

The trained troops are organized in naval commando battalions, which are specifically deployed in the Arabian Sea, Bab al-Mandab, and the Red Sea to disrupt maritime navigation of commercial ships, to attack ports, conduct ship hijackings, and plant mines, among other things.

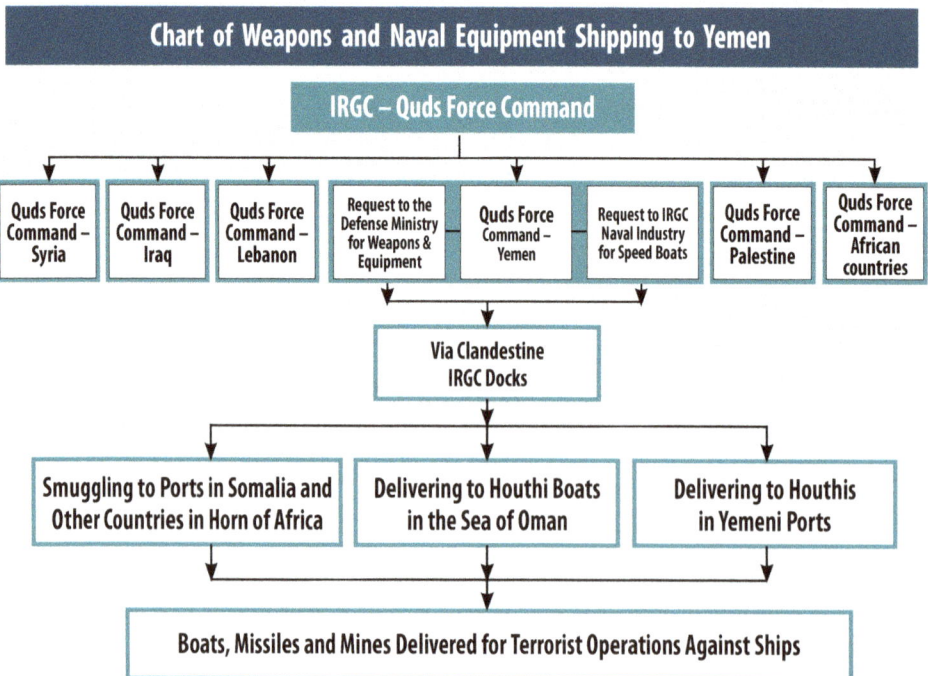

Chart of Weapons and Naval Equipment Shipping to Yemen

IRGC – Quds Force Command

- Quds Force Command – Syria
- Quds Force Command – Iraq
- Quds Force Command – Lebanon
- Request to the Defense Ministry for Weapons & Equipment
- Quds Force Command – Yemen
- Request to IRGC Naval Industry for Speed Boats
- Quds Force Command – Palestine
- Quds Force Command – African countries

Via Clandestine IRGC Docks

- Smuggling to Ports in Somalia and Other Countries in Horn of Africa
- Delivering to Houthi Boats in the Sea of Oman
- Delivering to Houthis in Yemeni Ports

Boats, Missiles and Mines Delivered for Terrorist Operations Against Ships

Quds Force arms smuggling network

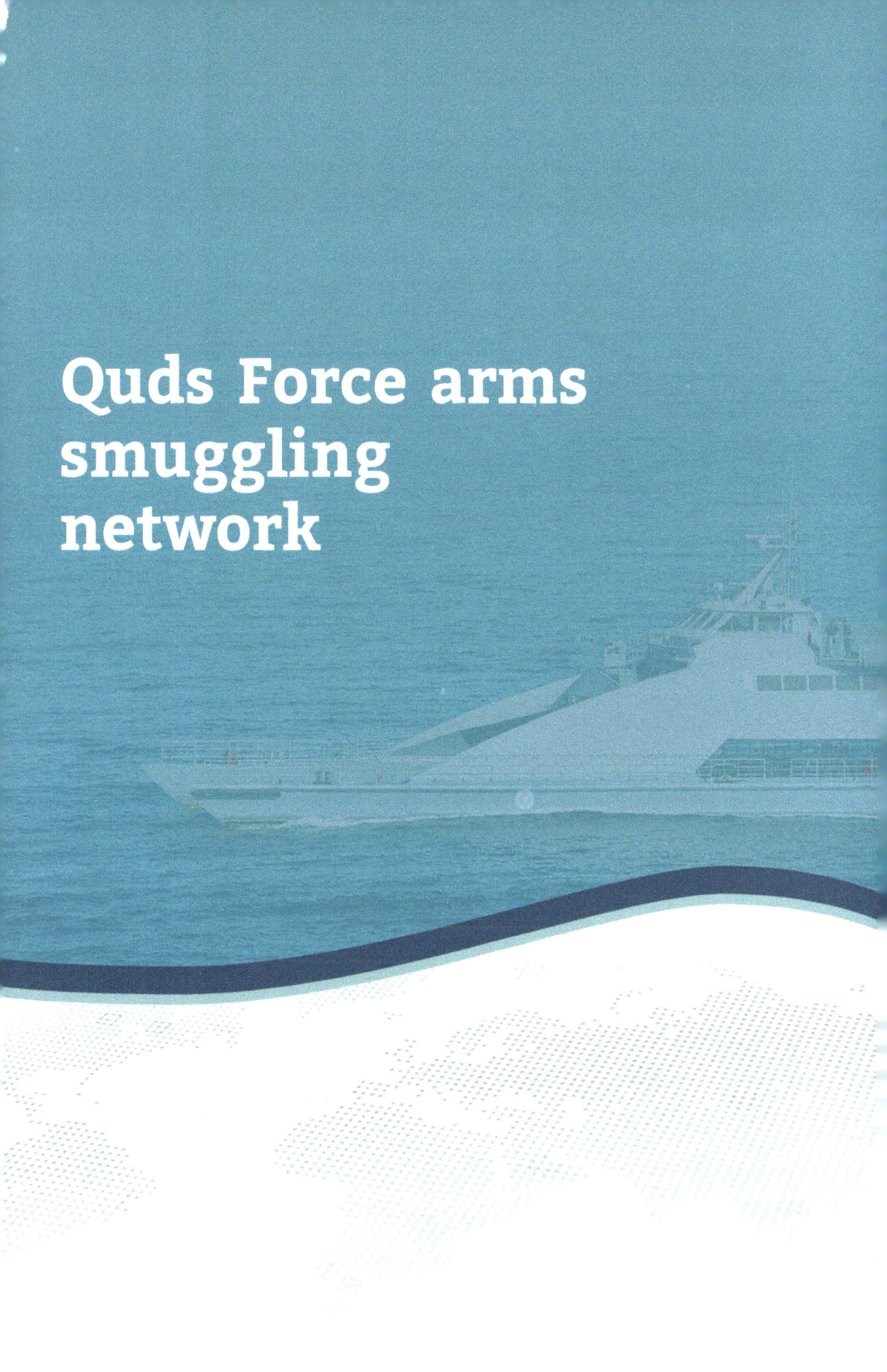

The Quds Force has set up a smuggling network to provide weapons and equipment to its proxies for naval attacks. One of the methods of transferring weapons to Yemen is to use third countries such as Somalia. The weapons are first loaded onto boats which move to Somalia's coasts, where they are unloaded. The weapons are then loaded onto smaller boats and sent to Yemen. Another method, also used by drug traffickers, is to hide weapons in other shipments or on board the ship itself:

- ▶ On August 13, 2019, some fenders were attached to a ship at the Bushehr wharf two days before the ship departed. Some of these fenders were 6m long. The Quds Force had hidden weapons and other military equipment inside them. Initially, the ship left Bushehr for loading at Lavan Island, but in the end no precise information was obtained about its ultimate destination.

- ▶ The regime uses fenders in other ways, as well. In one example, the fender is anchored and released with a long rope into the water in order to avoid detection. The fenders are equipped with GPS signals and styrofoam buoys on the surface of the water. A ship with a specific route carries the fenders and leaves them at a predetermined location, so that a second ship can find them with GPS, pick up the cargo and transport it to the final destination.

Fenders

Secret weapons transfers to the Houthis

One of the means that the IRGC uses for smuggling weapons to Yemen is small boats along the coasts of the Sea of Oman. One of the most important ports used for this purpose is Bandar-e-Jask in the Sea of Oman.

For example, according to reports obtained from the MEK network inside Iran, on May 27, 2020, a launch full of light weapons stopped two miles from the Jask pier. The operating crew were Yemeni. An IRGC officer would deliver food to this dinghy from the pier. The boat stayed in waiting for several days before ensuring a secure route to Oman or the United Arab Emirates.

According to several reports received in Fall 2021 from various sources in Iran's southern provinces, the IRGC has forcibly enlisted a number of local owners of cargo launches to deliver weapons to the Houthis in the Gulf of Aden.

According to one report, one local mariner had to make a 12-day round trip to deliver weapons from the shores of Makran to the Gulf of Aden, where the weapons were off loaded by the Houthis onto their own boats about 10 miles off the Yemeni coast. The IRGC provided the GPS coordinates of the loaded launch to the Houthis using mobile phones.

Another means used by the IRGC to deliver weapons to the Houthis involves confiscating the fishing boats of locals in the impoverished provinces of Hormozgan and Sistan & Baluchestan under various pretexts.

The independent command headquarters of the IRGC Navy, called Imamat Garrison, as well as the command headquarters of the 2nd naval region are located at Bandar-e-Jask.

Imamat Garrison is two kilometers to the east of the port city of Jask, and adjacent to Bahl village. The IRGC has taken over the

The port city of Jask in the Sea of Oman is home to Imamat Garrison, the base of the independent command headquarters of the IRGC Navy

surrounding area up to 3 kilometers from Imamat Garrison and has declared the area off limits to ordinary citizens.

The commander of Imamat Garrison is currently IRGC Col. Abbas Khaksari, who replaced his predecessor, IRGC Col. Teymour Paydareh. Over the past two years, the IRGC Navy has strengthened its command headquarters in Jask and set up three Bassij naval bases. IRGC Col. Ali Alinejad is the commander of the Bassij naval base.

The attacks on two oil tankers on June 13, 2019 near Jask were conducted by the IRGC Naval command. This attack was carried out by special operations units of the IRGC Navy, in cooperation with Imamat Garrison. At the time of this attack, IRGC Col. Paydareh was the commander of Imamat Garrison; his deputy at the time was IRGC Col. Jafari. The commander of the garrison's combat intelligence was IRGC officer Zare'ei.

In addition, the attack on an American drone on June 20, 2019, which brought down the drone, was carried out by the anti-aircraft unit at Bandar-e-Jask.

IRGC's secret docks for smuggling weapons and military equipment

In 1981, during the Iran-Iraq War, on Khomeini's orders and based on recommendations by the Revolutionary Council and the War Council, plans were drawn up for a number of piers to be built for the IRGC, to enable it to obtain weapons and other logistical or technical needs without being detected regionally or even by the people and press inside Iran.

In 1982, Khomeini gave the go-ahead for the secret docks to be built. Referred to as the Bahman Docks, the aim was to have neither government nor customs supervision over them. In addition, they were to be built and operated without the knowledge of international organizations.

After the end of the war and during Ali Khamenei's tenure as the regime's Supreme Leader, there was a renewed emphasis on the docks, used by the IRGC and the Khatam al-Anbiya Garrison to pursue their economic activities on a large scale, including to circumvent sanctions, and additionally to smuggle oil and petrochemical products. Currently, the Quds Force uses these docks to send weapons and military equipment, including missiles and UAVs, to its proxy forces in the region, including the Houthis in Yemen.

Implications

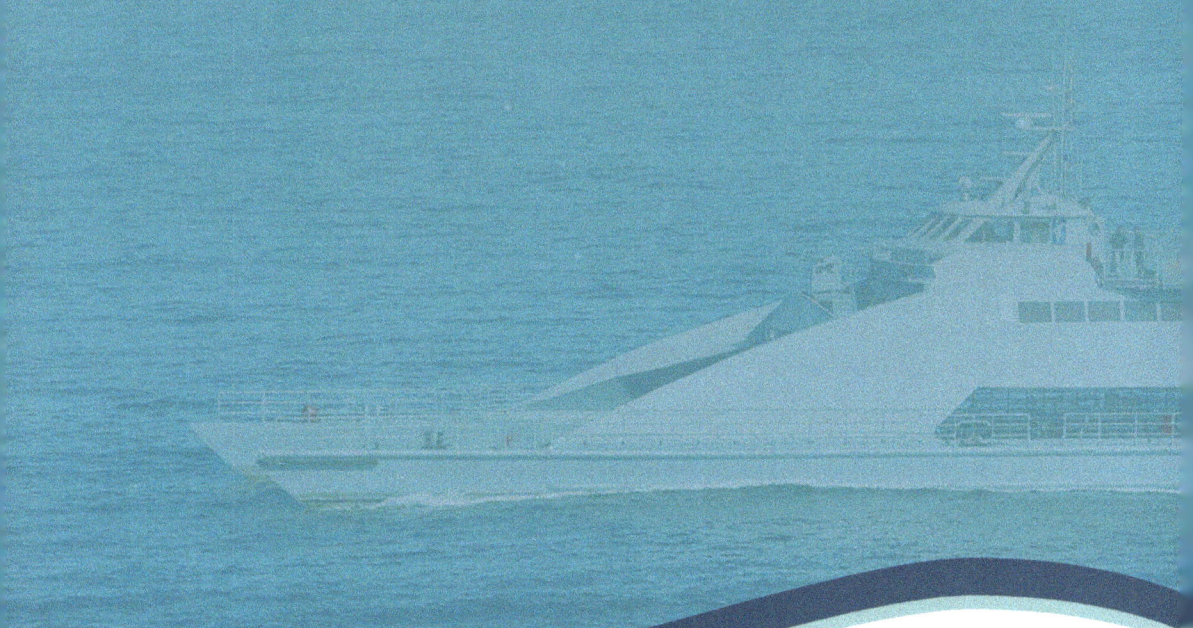

1. The Quds Force, as the IRGC's extraterritorial arm for terrorism, has launched plans to form proxy naval units, especially in Yemen. The command headquarters of the Quds Force in Yemen recruits Houthi forces for this purpose and sends them to Iran for training. These trained Houthis are then sent back to Yemen and organized in naval units.

2. The Quds Force has equipped the Houthis with speedboats, missiles, mines, and other weapons. It employs tactics that utilize speedboats and asymmetric warfare — similar to those used by the IRGC's Navy in the Persian Gulf — to expand conflicts into the Arabian Sea, Bab al-Mandab, and the Red Sea. Many terrorist operations in this region targeting foreign and Arab ships have been carried out by these naval units affiliated with the Quds Force.

3. In this way, the Iranian regime covers its tracks, and pursues its agenda under the shadow of the Houthi war in the region.

4. Since early 2021, and more so since August 2021, when Ebrahim Raisi took office as the new president of the Iranian regime, Tehran has stepped up its maritime terrorist operations using its foreign mercenaries, especially the Houthis. In fact, the destructive intervention of the Quds Force in the region has intensified, as have Tehran's UAV and missile attacks.

5. This escalation of maritime violence is in line with Tehran's stepped-up drone attacks against the Persian Gulf countries, as well as its nuclear defiance.

6. The continued offers of concessions by Western countries and lack of accountability for the Iranian regime's terrorist operations and its killings at home, have emboldened Tehran to step up its defiant behavior, creating mayhem in the region.

7. The billions of dollars plundered from Iran's national wealth

that the regime received from the easing of sanctions in the context of the nuclear deal have been expropriated to build and produce weapons, fund and train proxies in order to wage maritime terror operations, and export regional terrorism and warmongering. This is while a vast majority of the Iranian people live below the poverty line.

8. Since December 2017, there have been eight major uprisings, as well as successive protests by various sectors of Iranian society demanding fundamental change. Tehran's latest game plan to create terrorist naval units and step up regional mayhem is intended to project power and cover its fundamental weakness inside Iran. The regime hopes that this image will provide additional leverage internationally and domestically.

9. Regardless of what the Iranian regime might do with its nuclear weapons program and its negotiations with the P5+1, Tehran must be held accountable for its proxy wars in the region, its terrorism, its development of ballistic missiles, and its egregious violations of human rights and suppression of its own citizens engaged in ongoing uprisings.

10. This new information is added evidence that none of the sanctions against the regime should be lifted. To the contrary, additional sanctions are warranted as a result of the Iranian regime's escalation of violence in the region and stepped up repression at home.

List of publications

List of Publications by the National Council of Resistance of Iran, U.S. Representative Office

IRGC's Rising Drone Threat

A Desperate Regime's Ploy to Project Power, Incite War

December 2021, 70 pages

This book provides details of the most important organs of production, use and export of UAVs by the IRGC as well as 15 front companies used to provide parts.

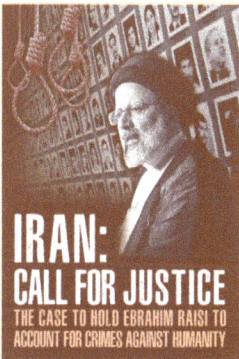

IRAN: Call for Justice

The Case to Hold Ebrahim Raisi to Account for Crimes Against Humanity

September 2021, 108 pages

This manuscript makes the case for bringing the clerical regime's president Ebrahim Raisi to justice before an international tribunal for the 1988 massacre, a clear case of crimes against humanity.

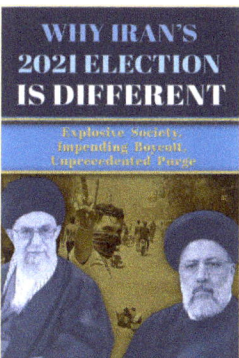

Why Iran's 2021 Election Is Different:

Explosive Society, Impending Boycott, Unprecedented Purge

May 2021, 80 pages

This report highlights the difference between the 2021 election and all prior 12 presidential elections in Iran.

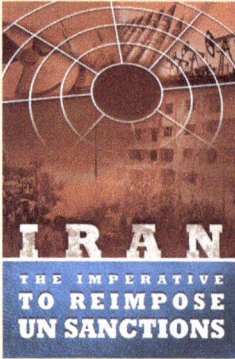

IRAN - The Imperative to Reimpose UN Sanctions

August 2020, 108 pages

This report shows how the Iranian regime is involved in procuring and manufacturing weapons and military equipment with the objective of exporting terrorism and warmongering, regional meddling by sending weapons and missiles to expand terrorist attacks, and resorts to terrorism.

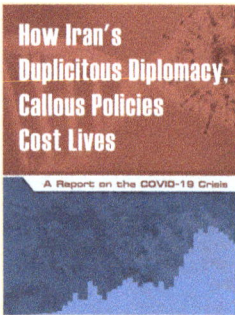

How Iran's Duplicitous Diplomacy, Callous Policies Cost Lives

A Report on the COVID-19 Crisis

April 2020, 84 pages

This report seeks to show that the Iranian Foreign Ministry's campaign to lift sanctions is replete with lies and misleading claims, with the goal of cynically exploiting the coronavirus pandemic to the regime's benefit In effect, the mullahs are causing the death of thousands of Iranians to preserve their own rule.

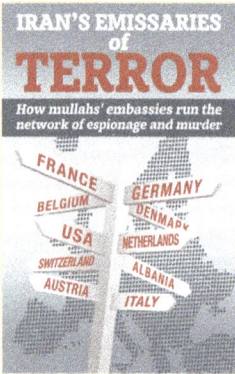

Iran's Emissaries of Terror

June 2019, 208 pages

This book explains the extent to which Tehran's embassies and diplomats are at the core of both the planning and execution of international terrorism targeting Iranian dissidents, as well as central to Tehran's direct and proxy terrorism against other countries.

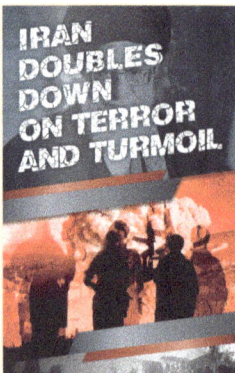

Iran Doubles Down on Terror and Turmoil

November 2018, 63 pages

This book examines the regime's political and economic strategy, which revolves around terrorism and physical annihilation of opponents. Failing to quell growing popular protests, Tehran has bolstered domestic suppression with blatant terrorism and intimidation.

Iran Will Be Free:
Speech by Maryam Rajavi
September 2018, 54 pages

Text of a keynote speech delivered by Mrs. Maryam Rajavi on June 30, 2018, at the Iranian Resistance's grand gathering in Paris, France explaining the path to freedom in Iran and what she envisions for future Iran.

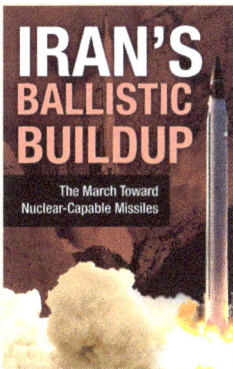

Iran's Ballistic Buildup:
The March Toward Nuclear-Capable Missiles
May 2018, 136 pages

This manuscript surveys Iran's missile capabilities, including the underlying organization, structure, production, and development infrastructure, as well as launch facilities and the command centers. The book exposes the nexus between the regime's missile activities and its nuclear weapons program, including ties with North Korea.

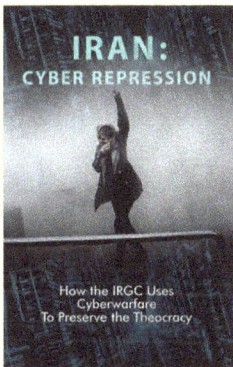

Iran: Cyber Repression: How the IRGC Uses Cyberwarfare to Preserve the Theocracy
February 2018, 70 pages

This manuscript demonstrates how the Iranian regime, under the supervision and guidance of the IRGC and the Ministry of Intelligence and Security (MOIS), have employed new cyberwarfare and tactics in a desperate attempt to counter the growing dissent inside the country.

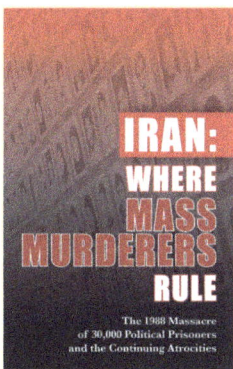

Iran: Where Mass Murderers Rule: The 1988 Massacre of 30,000 Political Prisoners and the Continuing Atrocities
November 2017, 161 pages

Iran: Where Mass Murderers Rule is an expose of the current rulers of Iran and their track record in human rights violations. The book details how 30,000 political prisoners fell victim to politicide during the summer of 1988 and showcases the egregious political extinction of a group of people.

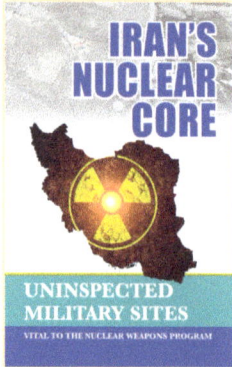

Iran's Nuclear Core: Uninspected Military Sites, Vital to the Nuclear Weapons Program

October 2017, 52 pages

This book details how the nuclear weapons program is at the heart of, and not parallel to, the civil nuclear program of Iran. The program has been run by the Islamic Revolutionary Guards Corp (IRGC) since the beginning, and the main nuclear sites and nuclear research facilities have been hidden from the eyes of the United Nations nuclear watchdog.

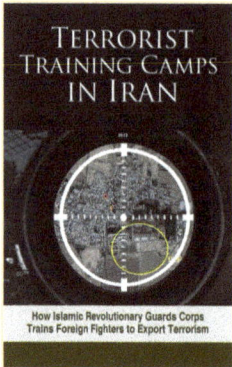

Terrorist Training Camps in Iran: How Islamic Revolutionary Guards Corps Trains Foreign Fighters to Export Terrorism

June 2017, 56 pages

The book details how Islamic Revolutionary Guards Corps trains foreign fighters in 15 various camps in Iran to export terrorism. The IRGC has created a large directorate within its extraterritorial arm, the Quds Force, in order to expand its training of foreign mercenaries as part of the strategy to step up its meddling abroad in Syria, Iraq, Yemen, Bahrain, Afghanistan and elsewhere.

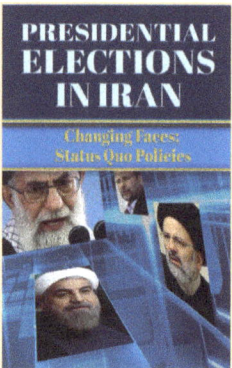

Presidential Elections in Iran: Changing Faces; Status Quo Policies

May 2017, 78 pages

The book reviews the past 11 presidential elections, demonstrating that the only criterion for qualifying as a candidate is practical and heartfelt allegiance to the Supreme Leader. An unelected vetting watchdog, the Guardian Council makes that determination.

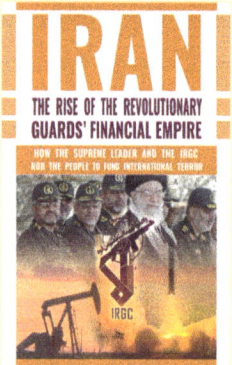

The Rise of Iran's Revolutionary Guards' Financial Empire: How the Supreme Leader and the IRGC Rob the People to Fund International Terror

March 2017, 174 pages

This study shows how ownership of property in various spheres of the economy is gradually shifted from the population writ large towards a minority ruling elite comprised of the Supreme Leader's office and the IRGC, using 14 powerhouses, and how the money ends up funding terrorism worldwide.

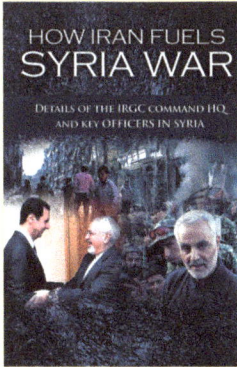

How Iran Fuels Syria War: Details of the IRGC Command HQ and Key Officers in Syria

November 2016, 74 pages

This book examines how the Iranian regime has effectively engaged in the military occupation of Syria by marshaling 70,000 forces, including the Islamic Revolutionary Guard Corps (IRGC) and mercenaries from other countries into Syria; is paying monthly salaries to over 250,000 militias and agents to prolong the conflict; and divided the country into 5 zones of conflict, establishing 18 command, logistics and operations centers.

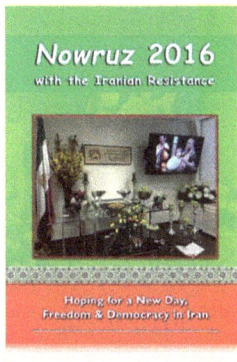

Nowruz 2016 with the Iranian Resistance: Hoping for a New Day, Freedom and Democracy in Iran

April 2016, 36 pages

This book describes Iranian New Year, Nowruz celebrations at the Washington office of Iran's parliament-in-exile, the National Council of Resistance of Iran. The yearly event marks the beginning of spring. It includes select speeches by dignitaries who have attended the NCRIUS Nowruz celebrations.

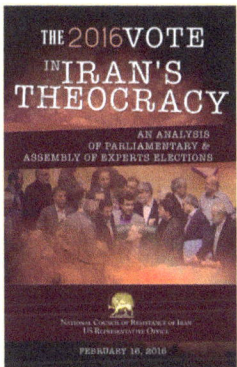

The 2016 Vote in Iran's Theocracy: An analysis of Parliamentary & Assembly of Experts Elections

February 2016, 70 pages

This book examines all the relevant data about the 2016 Assembly of Experts as well as Parliamentary elections ahead of the February 2016 elections. It looks at the history of elections since the revolution in 1979 and highlights the current intensified infighting among the various factions of the Iranian regime.

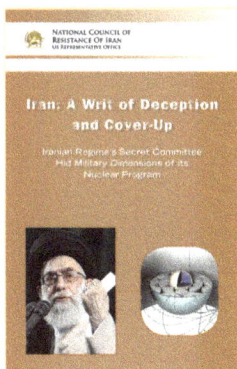

IRAN: A Writ of Deception and Cover-up: Iranian Regime's Secret Committee Hid Military Dimensions of its Nuclear Program

February 2016, 30 pages

The book provides details about a top-secret committee in charge of forging response to the International Atomic Energy Agency (IAEA) regarding the Possible Military Dimensions (PMD) of Tehran's nuclear program, including those related to the detonators called EBW (Exploding Bridge Wire), an integral part of developing an implosion type nuclear device.

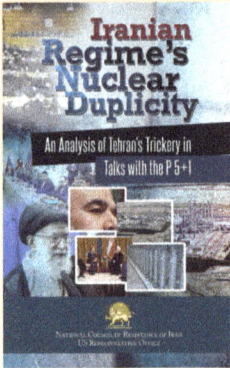

Iranian Regime's Nuclear Duplicity: An Analysis of Tehran's Trickery in Talks with the P5+1

January 2016, 74 pages

This book examines Iran's behavior throughout the negotiations process in an effort to inform the current dialogue on a potential agreement. Drawing on both publicly available sources and those within Iran, the book focuses on two major periods of intense negotiations with the regime: 2003-2004 and 2013-2015.

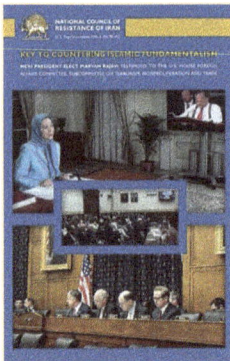

Key to Countering Islamic Fundamentalism: Maryam Rajavi? Testimony To The U.S. House Foreign Affairs Committee

June 2015, 68 pages

Testimony before U.S. House Foreign Affairs Committee's subcommittee on Terrorism, non-Proliferation, and Trade discussing ISIS and Islamic fundamentalism. The book contains Maryam Rajavi's full testimony as well as the question and answer by representatives.

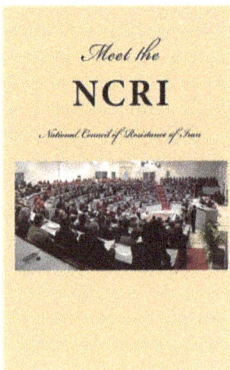

Meet the National Council of Resistance of Iran

June 2014, 150 pages

Meet the National Council of Resistance of Iran discusses what NCRI stands for, what its platform is, and why a vision for a free, democratic, secular, non-nuclear republic in Iran would serve world peace.

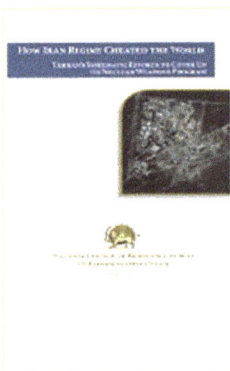

How Iran Regime Cheated the World: Tehran's Systematic Efforts to Cover Up its Nuclear Weapons Program

June 2014, 50 pages

The monograph discusses the Iranian regime's report card as far as it relates to being transparent when addressing the international community's concerns about the true nature and the ultimate purpose of its nuclear program.

About the NCRI-US

The National Council of Resistance of Iran-US Representative Office (NCRI-US) acts as the Washington office for Iran's parliament-in-exile, the National Council of Resistance of Iran, which is dedicated to the establishment of a democratic, secular, non-nuclear republic in Iran.

NCRI-US, registered as a non-profit tax-exempt organization, has been instrumental in exposing the nuclear weapons program of Iran, including the sites in Natanz and Arak, the biological and chemical weapons program, as well as the ambitious ballistic missile and drone programs.

NCRI-US has also exposed the terrorist network of the regime, including its involvement in the bombing of Khobar Towers in Saudi Arabia, the Jewish Community Center in Argentina, its fueling of sectarian violence in Iraq and Syria, and its malign activities in other parts of the Middle East.

With information gathered by the MEK intelligence network inside Iran, NCRI-US has also revealed crucial information about the vast financial empire run by the IRGC and Khamenei.

Our office has provided information on the human rights violations, extensive anti-government demonstrations, and the movement for democratic change in Iran.

Visit our website at www.ncrius.org

You may follow us on	twitter	@ncrius
Follow us on	facebook	NCRIUS
You can also find us on	Instagram	NCRIUS
Watch us on YouTube	You Tube	NCRI US